ATMOSPHERE AND WEATHER

WEATHER AND CLIMATE

ATMOSPHERE AND WEATHER

Terry Jennings

Evans

First published 2005 by Evans Brothers Limited
2A Portman Mansions
Chiltern Street
London W1U 6NR

British Library Cataloguing in Publication Data

Jennings, Terry J.
  Atmosphere and weather. - (Weather and climate)
  1.Atmosphere - Juvenile literature 2.Weather - Juvenile
  literature 3.Meteorology - Juvenile literature
  4.Climatology - Juvenile literature
  I.Title
  551.5'24

ISBN 0237527464

Designer: Giraffic Design
Editor: Mary-Jane Wilkins
Illustrator: Graham Rosewarne
Series consultant: Steve Watts

Picture acknowledgements
Ecoscene: page 6, 7, 9 (top), 43 (middle), 44 (middle), 45
Terry Jennings: page 2, 4, 11, 12, 15, 16, 21, 22, 24, 36, 37,
39 (top), 43 (top)
Oxford Scientific: front cover, page 14, 19 (middle), 20, 23,
28, 32, 33, 34 (bottom), 35, 38, 41 (bottom), 44 (middle)
Science Photo Library: page 9. 15 (bottom), 31, 34 (top),
39 (bottom), 41 (top), 42

Contents

The importance of weather

1

People have always been interested in the weather because of its huge effect on our lives. The weather determines not only the type of houses we live in, but also the clothes we wear when we go out, and whether we can play our favourite sport.

Ships' captains, fishermen, airline pilots and motorists need to know about weather conditions so that they can travel safely. The weather also affects the types of plants and animals that share our part of the Earth, the foods we eat and the farming methods used to produce that food. Farmers, perhaps more than anyone else, are at the mercy of the weather because an unexpected frost, hailstorm or drought can destroy a tender crop, while too much rain can cause destructive floods.

The Sun's heat powers all of our weather. The weather in the middle latitudes is so changeable that many holidaymakers travel long distances to spend time in warm sunshine, such as here in Benidorm, Spain.

*Drought can devastate
tender crops. This field
of sweetcorn or maize was
destroyed by the drought
that affected large parts of
the United Kingdom in 1995.*

What is weather?

Weather is the condition of the air at a certain time or over a brief
period of time. Weather includes the temperature, the pressure of
the air, the strength and direction of the wind, visibility, how much
moisture the air contains, the cloud cover and the amount and type
of precipitation. These and other factors combine to give us fine, sunny
days or cold, wet ones. The study of weather is called meteorology.
Meteorologists study the atmosphere, the thin layer of air around
the Earth, and the causes of weather. Some meteorologists work at
weather stations, collecting information about atmospheric movements
of all kinds, while others work at forecasting centres.

Weather and climate

Climate differs from weather, because climate is the average or usual
weather of a place over a long period of time. Climatologists study the
Earth's climates and how they affect plants and animals, including
people. They are interested in past and present climatic changes.
They also investigate how human activities affect world climates.

Air and atmosphere

The atmosphere is a thin layer of air surrounding the Earth. Air itself
is a mixture of gases – roughly four-fifths nitrogen and one-fifth oxygen,
with traces of carbon dioxide, argon and other gases such as xenon,
neon and krypton. There is also water in the atmosphere in the form
of the invisible gas water vapour, and as tiny water droplets and ice
crystals in clouds.

Pressure		Height
0.01 mb	THERMOSPHERE or IONOSPHERE	110 km
		100 km
	Mesopause	90 km
0.1 mb		80 km
	MESOSPHERE	70 km
1.0 mb		60 km
	Stratopause	50 km
		40 km
10 mb	STRATOSPHERE	30 km
	weather balloon	
		20 km
	Tropopause	
100 mb		
Mount Everest		10 km
	TROPOSPHERE	
1000 mb		

-80°   -60°   -40°   -20°   0°   20°

Temperature in °C

Atmospheric layers

The atmosphere is between 160 and 320 km thick and is made up of several layers. These extend from the Earth and fade out into space. All our weather occurs in the layer of the atmosphere nearest the Earth's surface. This layer, called the troposphere, extends up to about 8 km near the poles and to 16 km near the Equator. The troposphere contains 80 per cent of all the gases in the atmosphere. The temperature decreases with height in the troposphere. This is because the atmosphere receives its heat not directly from the Sun, but indirectly from the surface of the Earth.

The layer above the troposphere is called the stratosphere. This layer, which extends up to about 50 km, contains about 19 per cent of all the gases in the atmosphere. In the stratosphere the temperature is higher because it contains the ozone layer. The ozone layer absorbs most of the Sun's harmful ultraviolet radiation, preventing it from reaching the Earth. Long-distance jet aircraft fly in the stratosphere at heights of about 10,000m, where they are above the weather and the air is still.

In the topmost layer of the atmosphere, the exosphere, there are almost no gases and here the atmosphere merges into space.

Air pressure

Air has weight and it presses on things in all directions with a force called air pressure, or atmospheric pressure. Over one square metre, the weight of air pressing down is heavier than a large elephant. Air pressure is greatest near the ground and decreases with height. At 10,000m above the ground, where jet aircraft fly, the air pressure is very low and the weight of air pressing down on the aircraft is less. Because there is less air and oxygen, aircraft cabins have to be pressurized so that the passengers and crew can breathe. The air pressure inside the aircraft is roughly the same as at ground level.

The Earth's atmosphere is made up of several layers. All our weather occurs within the lowest layer, the troposphere.

Depressions and anticyclones

Air pressure plays an important part in creating different weather conditions, especially winds. Low atmospheric pressure areas, or depressions, cause unsettled weather in the British Isles, Europe and many other parts of the middle latitudes. The other main air system in these latitudes is an anticyclone. This is an area of high pressure. Anticyclones are associated with settled weather. In summer, there may be a succession of hot, sunny days. But in winter, anticyclones may bring cold weather and fogs.

Measuring air pressure

Air pressure is measured with a barometer. The first barometers were made from a long vertical tube, closed at the top and opening at the bottom into a dish. Both the dish and the tube contained mercury. There was no air above the column of mercury; instead there was an empty space, or vacuum. As the air pressure increased it pushed down on the mercury in the dish, forcing it up the tube, where its height was measured against a scale. When the air pressure fell, the height of the mercury also fell. Air pressure is measured in units called millibars. The average pressure at sea level is 1013.25 millibars.

A barometer measures the air pressure. This barometer, called a barograph, records the air pressure automatically on a revolving drum.

More portable than a mercury barometer, and easier to use, is an aneroid barometer. This has a needle and dial above a sealed metal box containing a partial vacuum. When air presses against the metal box, a series of springs and levers move the needle. The greater the air pressure, the further the needle moves in a clockwise direction. The lower the air pressure, the further the needle moves anticlockwise.

THE FIRST BAROMETER

Italian Evangelista Torricelli made the first barometer in 1644. He filled a metre-long glass tube with mercury and held the open end under the surface of a bowl of mercury. The level of the mercury in the tube dropped to about 80 cm, leaving a vacuum at the top. Torricelli realised that the weight, or pressure, of the air on the mercury in the bowl held up the column of mercury in the tube.

The French mathematician Blaise Pascal was interested in Torricelli's work. In 1648 Pascal proved that the atmosphere has weight (or pressure) by sending his brother-in-law up a mountain with a barometer. The level of mercury in the barometer tube dropped the higher he climbed.

The power of the Sun

2

The weather on Earth varies enormously from
place to place at any particular moment. Different
places have sunshine, sweltering heat, thick cloud,
freezing conditions, blinding snow, howling gales
or torrential rain. The Sun powers all these
changes in the weather.

Heat from the Sun

Temperature is the most important factor affecting the weather and
this is controlled by the Sun. Temperature is a measure of heat or cold,
and the amount of heat that reaches the Earth's surface varies from
place to place. Generally the Sun's heat is greatest around the Equator,
but decreases towards the poles.

The atmosphere absorbs some of the Sun's heat and, because the
Earth's surface is curved, the Sun's rays have to pass through a greater
thickness of atmosphere near the poles. As a result, less heat reaches
the ground near the poles, and so they are much cooler than the areas
near the Equator. The Sun's rays are also spread over a larger area
near the poles, again because of the curvature of the Earth's surface,
and so they have less warming power.

**THE EFFECT OF THE CURVATURE
OF THE EARTH ON THE SUN'S RAYS**

Sun's rays

Sun's rays

Seasonal changes

There are seasonal differences in temperature in many parts of the world. As the Earth orbits the Sun, its axis is tilted by 23.5°, which means that the amount of heat received at most places varies according to the time of the year. This causes the seasons.

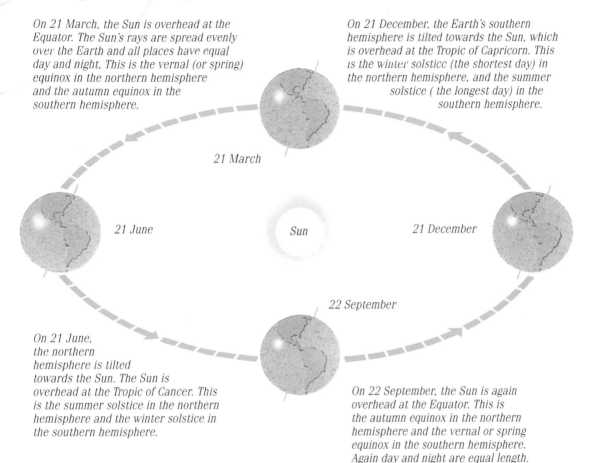

On 21 March, the Sun is overhead at the Equator. The Sun's rays are spread evenly over the Earth and all places have equal day and night. This is the vernal (or spring) equinox in the northern hemisphere and the autumn equinox in the southern hemisphere.

On 21 December, the Earth's southern hemisphere is tilted towards the Sun, which is overhead at the Tropic of Capricorn. This is the winter solstice (the shortest day) in the northern hemisphere, and the summer solstice (the longest day) in the southern hemisphere.

21 March

21 June

Sun

21 December

22 September

On 21 June, the northern hemisphere is tilted towards the Sun. The Sun is overhead at the Tropic of Cancer. This is the summer solstice in the northern hemisphere and the winter solstice in the southern hemisphere.

On 22 September, the Sun is again overhead at the Equator. This is the autumn equinox in the northern hemisphere and the vernal or spring equinox in the southern hemisphere. Again day and night are equal length.

In temperate climates, the four seasons are marked by changes to deciduous trees, as shown by this English hedgerow oak tree photographed in spring, summer, autumn and winter.

Temperature variations

Temperatures on Earth vary from place to place because of latitude and altitude. Temperatures are much higher near the Equator than near the poles. Over the Earth as a whole the temperature drops gradually as you move north or south away from the Equator. This is described as a gradual reduction of temperature with increasing latitude.

The Sun does not warm the air directly: it warms the Earth, which heats the air above it. As a result, the higher you go above the Earth the less the air is warmed. If you climb a mountain there is a noticeable drop in temperature as you move away from the source of heat. On average, the temperature falls 2°C for every 300m you climb. This reduction in temperature with altitude has several effects. The city of Quito, the capital of Ecuador, lies almost on the Equator in South America. But its average temperature is only 13°C because it lies in a narrow valley in the Andes Mountains, 2,820m above sea level.

Plant life is also affected by changes of temperature with altitude. For example, deciduous forests grow below 760m on Mount Washington in New Hampshire in the USA. Above 760m is mixed forest, which merges into coniferous forest at 980m. Between 1,220 and 1,520m small shrubs grow. The height above which trees will not grow is called the tree-line. The tops of the highest mountains, even near the Equator, are always snowy. The snow-line (the line above which snow does not melt in summer) is between 5,000 and 5,500m near the Equator, at 2,700m in the European Alps, and at sea level near the poles.

The height above which trees cannot grow on a mountain is called the tree-line. The tops of the highest mountains, such as these in the Austrian Alps, are permanently covered with snow.

The effect of land and sea

The nearness of an ocean or sea has a big effect on temperature. When the Sun's heat strikes land, only a very thin layer of soil and rock absorbs the heat. So the land warms up fast, but also loses heat fast. Over the oceans, the Sun's heat penetrates deeply and warms a greater volume. The oceans warm up slowly but hold their heat much longer.

Places near oceans and seas have a much smaller difference in temperature between summer and winter than places far inland. Edinburgh and Moscow are both about the same distance from the Equator. The average maximum temperature in Edinburgh in January is 6°C and in July 18°C. By contrast the average maximum in Moscow is –9°C in January and 23°C in July. Moscow is far from the sea, so summers there can be very hot, and the winters are severe. Edinburgh is close to the sea and has no extremes of temperature.

Cloud barriers

Clouds act as barriers to the Sun's rays. So the world's highest temperatures are recorded not in the cloudy regions near the Equator, but under the clear sunny skies of hot deserts further north or south. Clouds also reduce the loss of heat from the land, so cloudy regions have a small daily range of temperature, compared with the hot days and cold nights of the deserts. In Europe and North America, the lowest temperatures are recorded on winter nights when there are clear starlit skies and no clouds to reduce the loss of heat from the land.

Ocean currents

The waters of the oceans mix and circulate. Warm water from the tropics flows towards the poles, while cold water from the polar regions flows towards the Equator. Sometimes currents form a stream, such as the Gulf Stream. Most currents are caused by winds that blow in the same direction all the time. The Gulf Stream begins with warm (26-29°C) water near the Equator in the Gulf of Mexico. This flows up the east coast of the United States, warming the land. The Gulf Stream then flows across the Atlantic Ocean and fans out into the North Atlantic Drift. The warm air over them brings milder winters to parts of north-west Europe than you would expect for places so far north.

The main ocean currents in the North Atlantic. Cold currents are shown in blue and warm currents in red.

St Lawrence

Labrador Current

Arctic Circle

North Atlantic Drift

Gulf Stream

⟶ *Prevailing wind*

Huge waves on the coast of Southern California caused by an El Niño event in February 1998.

Warm winds

The winds which blow over warm ocean currents to the land are warmed by them. These winds carry moisture and often bring rain. Winds which blow over cold currents, such as the Labrador Current which flows south from the Arctic between Greenland and eastern Canada, are cool. They do not hold much moisture and so dry the land.

The effect of an ocean on the temperature is reduced as you travel away from it. The prevailing winds in the British Isles come from the south-west. They are formed over the Atlantic Ocean and warmed by the Gulf Stream and the North Atlantic Drift. They are relatively warm in winter and cool in summer, and produce similar temperatures over the British Isles. The prevailing winds on the eastern coast of the United States also come from the south-west, but they blow over the North American continent. So the eastern coast of the United States has hot summers, cold winters and a wide annual range of temperature.

The effect of relief

The shape of the Earth (its relief) also creates temperature differences. Vineyards and orchards are planted on the sides of valleys, rather than in the fertile soils in the bottom of the valleys. This is because heavy, cold air moves down the slopes and collects in valley bottoms. For similar reasons, Alpine villages are built on the north sides of valleys which run from east to west, so they receive more of the Sun's warmth. Mountains also provide shelter from cold winds.

The village of Rickmansworth to the north-west of London is in a frost hollow where cold air collects in the bottom of a valley. Here, temperatures can be 15°C lower than in central London 24 km away.

Measuring temperature

Air temperature is measured with a dry bulb thermometer. This narrow, sealed tube of glass has a bulb at one end. The mercury inside expands and contracts with changes in the air temperature.

Meteorologists record the highest and lowest temperature over every 24 hours with two special thermometers. The maximum thermometer records the highest. It is like a dry bulb thermometer, except that the glass tube narrows near the bulb. As the temperature rises, the mercury expands. When the temperature falls the mercury contracts, but the narrow tube prevents it going back into the bulb. The top of the mercury column shows the highest temperature since the thermometer was set.

The minimum thermometer measures the lowest temperature. It is filled with alcohol and has a small pin inside. This is carried towards the bulb as the temperature falls and the alcohol contracts. When the temperature rises again, the alcohol expands and the pin is left in the tube. The end of the pin furthest from the bulb marks the minimum temperature. These thermometers are mounted horizontally so that gravity does not affect the readings. Both are reset every day. A double-ended thermometer can also measure these temperatures. It contains mercury and has a small pin in each tube, to record the maximum and minimum temperature. They are reset after taking a reading.

The small pins in this double-ended maximum and minimum thermometer are reset by a push-button mechanism.

HOT AND COLD

The hottest place on Earth is El Azizia in the Libyan desert. On 13 September 1922, a temperature of 58°C was recorded. The world's lowest temperature, −89.2°C, was recorded at Vostok Scientific Station, Antarctica on 21 July 1983.

Sunshine recorders

Most seaside resorts record the sunshine they receive daily, often using a Campbell-Stokes sunshine recorder. Every day a light-sensitive card is fitted into the semi-circular frame. When the Sun shines, the glass ball mounted in front of the card focuses the Sun's rays so a mark is burned on the card. As the Earth turns, the burn mark moves along the card. None are made when the Sun is not shining. The card is marked in hours and parts of hours, which makes it easy to add up the length of time the Sun shone on any day.

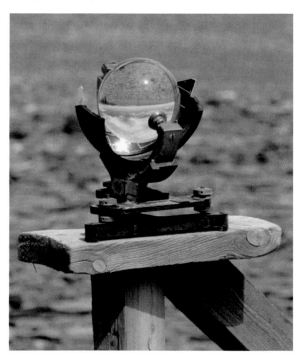

The Sun's rays pass through the glass sphere of a Campbell-Stokes sunshine recorder in the Hoggar Mountains of Algeria.

Wind

3

Wind is moving air. The Earth's atmosphere is always moving, and currents of air move from place to place as wind. We cannot see the wind but we can feel it. We can also see the effects of winds, for example when they rustle the leaves of trees, make branches sway, or make waves crash on the seashore.

Strong winds have pruned this hedge near the east coast of Norfolk, England, so that it is bent over in the direction of the prevailing wind.

Strong winds that nearly always blow from the same direction are called prevailing winds. In exposed areas you can tell the direction from which the prevailing wind blows. It prevents trees from growing upright, so they are bent over in the direction the wind blows.

Why do winds blow?

Winds blow from place to place because the Sun warms some parts of the Earth more than others. Air over warmer ground is also warmed. As the air increases in temperature it expands and so becomes less dense, or 'lighter'. Because it is 'lighter' than the surrounding air the warm air rises, in the same way that a hot-air balloon rises.

The rising warm air is replaced by cooler air moving in from the surrounding area. This creates winds close to the ground. When the rising warm air reaches the upper atmosphere it rushes to replace the sinking cooler air, so creating upper-level winds and completing the cycle.

Land and sea breezes

To understand how and why winds blow, think of a gentle wind, or breeze, near the coast. On a sunny morning by the coast the land heats up faster than the sea and it warms the air above it. The warmer air expands and begins to rise. This lowers the air pressure above the land, and so cooler air is drawn in from the sea, as a sea breeze.

Meanwhile, over the sea the air is still cool and sinking. This increases the air pressure over the sea. High in the sky, winds fed by the air rising over the land, blow out to sea to replace the sinking air. During the late evening of the same day, the direction of the winds is

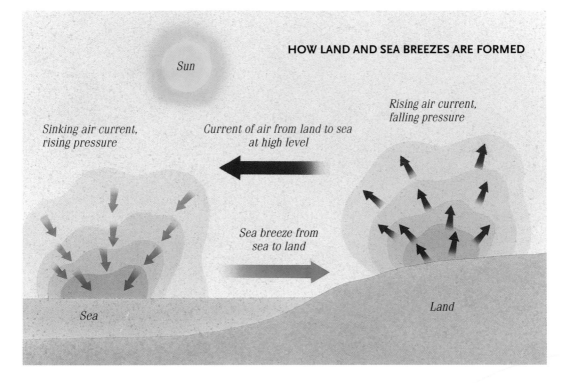

HOW LAND AND SEA BREEZES ARE FORMED

Sun

Rising air current, falling pressure

Sinking air current, rising pressure

Current of air from land to sea at high level

Sea breeze from sea to land

Land

Sea

reversed. This is because the sea keeps its warmth longer than the land. Air flowing away from the seashore is called a land breeze.

World winds

To the north of the Equator lies the Tropic of Cancer and, an equal distance south, lies the Tropic of Capricorn. The region between the two, known as the tropics, receives far more heat from the Sun than the areas outside it.

As the land near the Equator is heated, the hot air above it rises. As hot air is 'lighter', or less dense than cold air, the air pressure around the Equator is low. The hot air cools as it rises and eventually flows to the north and south. It sinks back to the Earth in the zones of high pressure about 30° north and south. These belts of calm or light winds are sometimes called the horse latitudes, although no one is sure where the name came from.

From the horse latitudes, winds called trade winds blow back towards the doldrums, the belt of calm air with high humidity and high temperatures near the Equator, while westerly winds blow towards the poles.

Above the Earth's poles, with their vast areas of ice and snow, the air is cooled. It sinks and spreads outwards. These cold winds are called polar easterlies and when they reach the Earth's middle latitudes (midway between the Equator and the poles), they meet warmer winds. The boundary where this happens is called the polar front. As the two sets of winds collide, they do not mix but instead produce frontal depressions (see page 30).

Prevailing winds

Trade winds, westerlies and polar easterlies are the world's prevailing winds. These winds do not blow in straight lines north-south. This is because the Earth spins on its axis and this spin produces the Coriolis effect, which throws winds sideways from their path. In the northern hemisphere winds are thrown to the right of their path, so that the trade winds north of the Equator blow from the north-east to the south-west. In the southern hemisphere the winds curve to the left.

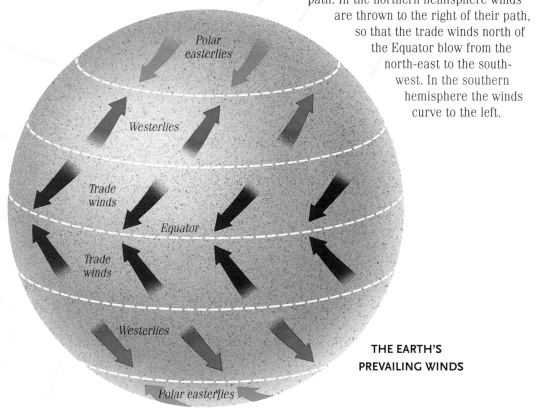

THE EARTH'S
PREVAILING WINDS

Other factors, such as mountain ranges and valleys, or friction with the land, also affect winds. In high and low pressure air systems (anticyclones and depressions), winds spiral around the centre, like bath water around an open plug hole.

Monsoon winds change direction according to the season. In summer these winds carry moisture evaporated from the sea. This moisture falls as rain on land areas in southern Asia. In winter the direction of the winds is reversed, and dry winds blow away from the land towards the sea. Like sea breezes, monsoon winds are the result of unequal heating of land and sea. In summer the land area of southern Asia heats up rapidly and low pressure results. Warm, moist winds sweep in from the sea as the summer monsoon. In winter the land areas of southern Asia lose heat rapidly. The low temperatures lead to very high pressure and cold, dry air moves away from the land towards the relatively warm air and low pressure over the sea.

Flooding caused by heavy rain during the summer monsoon season in Vietnam.

Hurricanes

You can see the full power of moving air in the violent storms we call hurricanes and tornadoes. Hurricanes begin over the warm waters of the Atlantic Ocean, where the temperature is over 27°C. Meteorologists believe that hurricanes form when the air is warmer than the surface of the ocean. The storms pick up vast amounts of energy and moisture as they rush towards the land.

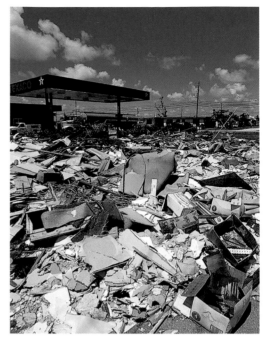

Hurricanes are among the most ferocious of windstorms and do widespread damage. This damage was caused by Hurricane Andrew when it hit Florida in August 1992.

A hurricane can measure 400 km across. Inside it the swirling mass of winds spiral upwards. At the centre, or eye, of a hurricane the skies are clear and the temperatures high. The calm eye may be 40 km across, but the strongest winds, with speeds of up to 350 kph are immediately around it. Hurricanes often travel over the Caribbean Islands and the mainland of North America. When this happens, high winds and torrential rain can cause massive damage to crops and property, and sometimes also kill people. Storms like this are known as typhoons in the China Sea, cyclones in the Bay of Bengal and willy-willies off the north-west coast of Australia.

HURRICANE NAMES

When a hurricane is first spotted meteorologists give it a name to identify it. The first hurricane of the season is given a name beginning with the letter 'A', the next 'B' and so on. This custom was first started by an Australian weather forecaster, Clement Wragge (1852-1922), who used names from the Bible. Since 1978 meteorologists have drawn up a list of alternate male and female names, in alphabetical order. Each new hurricane is given the next name on the list.

TORNADO ZONES

Some places have frequent tornadoes. The stretch of land that runs from the Gulf of Mexico, through the states of Texas, Oklahoma, Kansas, Nebraska and the Dakotas in the United States has so many tornadoes that it is known as tornado alley. It has about 700 tornadoes every year. They are caused by cold, dry air masses from Canada meeting warm, wet air from the Gulf of Mexico.

In a violent tornado the wind can reach speeds of over 800 kph. This brings massive destruction and can leave hundreds of people injured and homeless. This is the devastation left by a tornado which struck Saragosa, Texas in the United States in May 1997.

Tornadoes

Tornadoes are small, extremely powerful whirlwinds that form very suddenly. Every tornado is a violent, rapidly-twisting funnel of cloud that stretches from a storm cloud to the ground. In the United States, where tornadoes are common, they are often called twisters. Tornadoes can be as small as a few metres or as big as 100m across and they travel over the land at speeds of 30 to 65 km/h. But inside a tornado are the highest wind speeds on Earth. These speeds can be over 800 km/h.

A tornado destroys everything in its path, which can extend for more than 200 km, before it uses up all its energy. On average, there are about 1,000 tornadoes in the United States every year, and they also happen regularly in parts of Canada, Argentina, China, Australia, South-West Asia and even Europe. In the United Kingdom there are between 15 and 30 tornadoes a year.

A tornado which forms over a lake or the sea is called a waterspout.

RAINING FROGS

From time to time people report seeing frogs, fish and other small animals falling from the sky during rainstorms. These animals were probably sucked up from ponds and rivers by small tornadoes, and then fell to the ground again with the rain.

THE BEAUFORT SCALE

We can estimate wind speed using the Beaufort Scale. This was developed in 1805 by Sir Francis Beaufort to estimate wind speed at sea. It was later extended to include exact wind speeds and adapted for use on land.

Beaufort number	Kilometres per hour	Wind description
0	Less than 1	Calm
1	1 – 5	Light air movement
2	6 – 11	Slight breeze
3	12 – 19	Gentle breeze
4	20 – 28	Moderate breeze
5	29 – 38	Fresh breeze
6	39 – 49	Strong breeze
7	50 – 61	Moderate gale (or high wind)
8	62 – 74	Gale
9	75 – 88	Strong gale
10	89 – 102	Storm
11	103 – 117	Violent storm
12	118 or more	Hurricane

Measuring wind speed and direction

Wind direction is shown by a wind vane or weather vane. This is an arrow that turns on a pivot. The tail of the arrow is larger than its head. When the wind strikes the tail, it turns the arrow to point in the direction from which the air is coming. This is used as the name of the wind, so that a westerly wind blows from the west. At airfields, a wind-sock is used to show not only wind direction but also to give an indication of wind speed. The more horizontal the sock is, the stronger the wind.

An anemometer gives an accurate measurement of wind speed. This instrument is usually mounted 10 metres up a pole or on a building, although hand-held versions are available. The three or four cups are attached to a spindle. As the wind blows the cups round, the spindle turns; the greater the wind force, the faster the cups turn. The spindle is coupled to a device for measuring the wind speed. Usually this is a dial like a car speedometer.

The cup anemometer, invented in 1846, measures and records wind speeds.

Water in the air

4

The atmosphere always contains the invisible gas water vapour. Most of this water vapour is in the troposphere, the lowest layer of the atmosphere. Water vapour is continuously formed as the Sun warms oceans, seas, lakes, rivers and other wet surfaces, and as water evaporates from plants.

Relative humidity

The temperature of the air determines how much water vapour it can hold. Warm air holds more water vapour than cold air. As a result, the air over hot deserts often contains much more water vapour than the air over cooler lands. But the water vapour in the hot air rarely condenses into visible water droplets, because the air has to cool below dew point before condensation occurs. Dew point is the temperature at which the air is saturated – that is, when the air contains all the water vapour that it can at that temperature. Meteorologists say that the air at dew point has a relative humidity of 100 per cent. The relative humidity is the ratio between the amount of water vapour in the air and the maximum amount that it can hold at that temperature.

WET ATMOSPHERE

Scientists estimate that at any one time the atmosphere contains about 15,470 trillion litres of water. Because of the pull of the Earth's gravity, nearly all this water is in the troposphere, the layer of the atmosphere closest to the Earth's surface.

Condensation

For water vapour in the air to become liquid water it must be cooled so that it condenses. Sometimes, when the Sun comes out after a summer shower, you see steam rising from a road. The Sun's heat turns water on the tarmac into water vapour. The colder air above the tarmac turns the water vapour back into the small water droplets we see as steam.

Below dew point, water vapour in the atmosphere condenses around tiny bits of dust, plant pollen or salt from the oceans to form droplets of water or tiny ice crystals. The droplets of water and ice crystals are so small that they remain suspended in the air. Masses of these particles form clouds in the air, and fog, mist and dew near the ground.

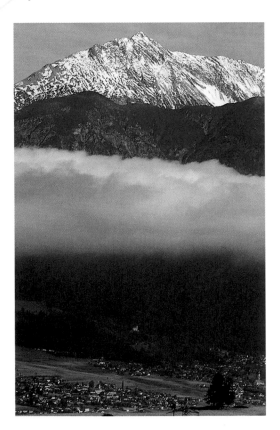

Advection fog (see page 23) in the Austrian Alps. Cool, dense air rolled down into the valley during the night and its moisture condensed into this blanket of fog.

Fog and mist

Fog and mist are clouds at ground level. They form in calm, clear weather. The most common kind of fog forms at night when the land in low-lying areas cools enough to bring the air above to its dew point. Water vapour in the cooling air condenses into water droplets. They are so light that they remain suspended in the air. The fog spreads slowly up from the ground and is called radiation fog. Radiation fog causes many aircraft and road accidents.

The other kind of fog, called advection fog, forms where a warm, moist wind blows over a cooler surface. Advection fog often forms in the harbour at San Francisco in the United States because warm, moist air from the south blows over cool ocean currents flowing down from the Arctic. Advection fog also forms in valleys. There air that has cooled and become denser during the night rolls down into a valley from the surrounding hills or mountains. Condensation then occurs, and the valley fills with fog.

In a mist we can see more than 1,000 metres but less than 2,000 metres. Fogs are thicker. In a fog, the visibility is less than 1,000 metres and it may drop to only a metre or so. Mist and fog formed by radiation usually clear quickly when the temperature rises. Advection fogs are slow to clear because they disperse only when there is a change in the conditions that caused them.

Dew drops

Dew is drops of water deposited on blades of grass, cobwebs, stones and other objects. Dew is formed under the same conditions as mist and fog except that the air is still. Then, only the lowest layer of the atmosphere is cooled. As the temperature of this layer falls below dew point, the water vapour in the air condenses and drops of water are deposited on the ground. You can see similar condensation on the outside of an ice-cold glass of drink. Dew often forms on grasses and other plants because their leaves give out moisture. As a result, the air next to the leaves has a high humidity and little cooling is needed to make the water vapour condense.

Dew is a thin coating of water droplets that condenses on spiders' webs, grass, stones and other surfaces, when the air is cooled below dew point.

On calm winter nights, air that touches the ground may be chilled so that the water vapour in it turns into ice crystals. The resulting layer of frost may be so thick that it looks like snow, as on the fruit and leaves of this ivy plant.

How frost is formed

Frost, like fog, forms on clear nights when there are no clouds to reduce heat loss from the Earth. For frost to form the temperature must drop to below freezing point (0°C). True frost, or hoar frost, is formed when a thin layer of moist air near the ground cools quickly to below freezing. The water vapour in the air forms ice crystals, without condensing to liquid water, or dew. The crystals coat any cold surface,

The water cycle

The water in the atmosphere, and the processes of evaporation and condensation are vital parts of the water cycle. Land plants and animals need a regular supply of fresh water and this is produced by the water cycle. The oceans and seas contain about 97 per cent of the

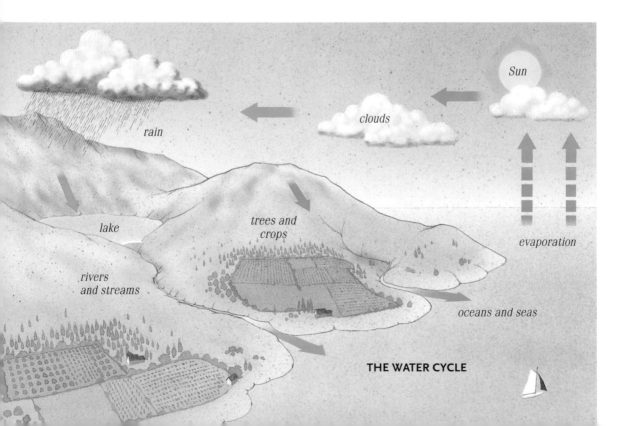

Sun

clouds

rain

lake

trees and crops

evaporation

rivers and streams

oceans and seas

THE WATER CYCLE

world's water and scientists believe that nearly 90 per cent of the water in the atmosphere comes from the oceans. The rest comes from seas, lakes, rivers, ponds, plants and other moist surfaces. Over the oceans, the Sun's rays evaporate water which becomes water vapour. Rising air currents carry it upwards. As it rises, it gradually cools. When it has cooled below dew point, the water vapour condenses into tiny droplets of water or minute crystals of ice that form clouds.

Winds blow the clouds towards the land. When they are forced to rise over mountains, this cools them further. They grow larger until the moisture in them falls as rain, snow, sleet or hail.

The main precipitation in temperate regions is rain. Some of the rain sinks into the soil and is taken up by the roots of plants. Most of this water evaporates from the plant leaves and returns to the air. Some water sinks through the soil into the rocks below. This water may return to the surface as springs, the sources of rivers, which carry water back to the sea, completing the water cycle.

In high mountain and polar regions, precipitation is mainly snow. The snow piles up and is compressed into ice. Large bodies of ice, ranging from huge ice sheets to glaciers, flow downhill towards the sea. On the coast, icebergs break off the ice sheets and glaciers. When the icebergs melt in the sea, they complete the water cycle in another way.

OVERHEATING
Very hot, humid weather conditions can be dangerous to people because sweat cannot evaporate from the body and cool it, so that heatstroke can result. This can lead to a person collapsing, going into a coma or even dying.

dry bulb thermometer *wet bulb thermometer*

muslin

water

Measuring humidity
Meteorologists measure relative humidity with two identical thermometers. One, the dry bulb thermometer, measures the air temperature. The other, the wet bulb thermometer, has a piece of wet muslin wrapped around its bulb and dipped in water. The lower the humidity of the air, the more water evaporates from the muslin. Evaporating water is cooling. You feel this when sweat evaporates from your skin after vigorous exercise and you start to shiver. Evaporation lowers the temperature of the wet bulb thermometer. The relative humidity is the difference in temperature between the thermometers.

If the wet and dry bulb readings are the same, the air is saturated and has a relative humidity of 100 per cent.

Absolute humidity measures the amount of water vapour in a given volume of air. The amount of water vapour the air can hold increases with temperature, so relative humidity is a more useful measurement.

WET AND DRY BULB THERMOMETER
The relative humidity is calculated from the difference in the temperatures shown by these wet and dry bulb thermometers.

Clouds

Clouds form when air is
cooled until the water vapour
condenses into water droplets.
These droplets are so small they
remain suspended in the air, forming
a cloud. If it is very cold, the vapour
freezes into clouds of tiny ice crystals.

All clouds are in the troposphere, usually up to about 16 km.
Here the temperature drops with height, so when moist air
rises it cools and clouds form. The temperature at the top of
the troposphere is well below freezing, at about −55°C. If the
atmosphere were completely clean no clouds would form
because there would be nothing for the water vapour to
condense on to. But the air is laden with minute floating
particles such as dust, soot, salt from the sea and plant
pollen. These allow water vapour in the air to condense.
Near the ground this forms fog and at higher levels, clouds.

Types of clouds

There are three main groups of clouds. The names of
high-level clouds include the words cirrus or cirro.
Medium-level clouds have names starting with alto.
Low-level clouds have various names. The words
nimbus or nimbo indicate rain-bearing clouds.
Great sheets of clouds have names that include
stratus or strato, meaning layer. Names for clouds
that look like fluffy heaps include the words cumulus
or cumulo, meaning a pile or heap.

High-level clouds

Clouds above 5,000m form a thin, feathery white
veil that does not completely blot out the Sun.
They are made of ice crystals, not water
droplets. There are three types.
　　In cirrus clouds the ice crystals
are drawn into feathery streaks
across the sky. They are also
called mare's tails.

Cumulonimbus

Stratus

Cirrus

Cirrostratus clouds are formed by ice crystals at high levels, making a layer of white cloud over large parts of the sky. If the Sun shines through, it has a halo. If the ice crystals are gathered into small clouds arranged in rows, they are called cirrocumulus.

Cirrocumulus

Medium-level clouds

These thicker, darker clouds form between 2,000 and 5,000m. Altostratus clouds have a thin layer of water droplets or ice crystals which the Sun or moon shines through weakly. They can blot out the Sun or moon.

Altocumulus are small cumulus at medium heights, often arranged in rows. The amount of blue sky between the clouds depends on their size and spacing. This kind of cloud cover may be called a mackerel sky.

Cirrostratus

Low-level clouds

There are five main types of clouds with bases below 2,000m. These are usually made entirely of water droplets.

Cumulus are thick clouds with flat bases and clearly outlined billows above. Small clouds with a lot of clear sky between them are fair-weather cumulus. Larger clouds are called towering cumulus and may bring rain.

Stratus is a simple layer of grey cloud with a base between ground level and about 2,000m. It may be many hundreds of metres thick but has no clear shape. Stratus clouds may bring drizzle or rain.

Altostratus

Stratocumulus consists of a large number of cumulus clouds with the same base level. The upper parts of the clouds are blurred. Individual clouds may appear in bands, between which the sun may shine.

Nimbostratus can be part of a continuous cloud layer from a few metres above ground to high-level clouds. These clouds produce rain in temperate climates. You can distinguish it from an ordinary stratus by the small masses of broken cloud called scud beneath its solid base.

Altocumulus

Cumulus clouds can tower to the top of the troposphere. Here the upward air currents weaken and strong winds blow across the top of the cloud, carrying the ice crystals horizontally. This creates an anvil shape at the top of the cloud. This is a thunder cloud and can produce very heavy rain, hail or snow, as well as thunder and lightning.

Stratocumulus

Cumulus

Nimbostratus

Rain

There could be no life without water. Farmers use water for growing crops and keeping livestock, and every human being needs water for drinking, cooking and sanitation. Industry also uses vast quantities of water. All this water comes ultimately from rain or other forms of precipitation.

How much rain?

Rainfall amounts vary enormously from region to region. Mawsynram, in the Meghalaya state of India, has a record-breaking total of 12m per year, while at the other end of the scale, less than 0.1 mm falls in the Atacama Desert in northern Chile.

Condensation and clouds

When moisture-laden air rises, it is heated by the Sun, and expands. As the air expands it becomes light and buoyant compared with the air around it. The less dense air rises by convection. As the air rises it begins to cool, and eventually the water vapour condenses to form clouds. The temperature at which this happens is called the dew point.

The clouds that sweep across the sky are made of billions of tiny water droplets or ice crystals, but they only give up their water when the conditions are right. For clouds to give up their moisture, they must rise in the atmosphere and be cooled still further. This can happen in different ways and each way produces a different type of rainfall.

Approaching storm clouds over Mahe Island in the Seychelles. In tropical areas such storms of heavy convectional rain may occur almost every day during the late afternoon in the rainy season.

▼▼▼
CAN WE MAKE IT RAIN?

Scientists discovered that silver iodide crystals grow when they collide with supercooled water droplets, in a similar way to ice crystals. They have tried to make rain fall where there is a shortage of water by flying over a cloud and 'seeding' it with ice crystals, or chemicals such as dry ice (solid carbon dioxide). But they have not always succeeded.

Convectional rain

Rain in tropical regions is called convectional rain. Here, high temperatures evaporate a lot of moisture from the land. The land heated by the hot Sun warms the air above it and the warm air rises. The strong upward air currents make the air cool and billowing cumulus clouds start to form. The clouds grow quickly to become towering cumulonimbus, which can be up to 20,000m high, made up of millions of tiny water droplets. As the warm air rises rapidly, the tiny water droplets collide and fuse into larger drops. Finally they become large enough to fall through the rising air as rain. The average diameter of a water droplet in a cloud is 0.02 mm. The average diameter of a raindrop is 2 mm – 100 times larger.

Some raindrops never reach the ground. They evaporate in the warm air beneath the cloud. This is why the bottom of some clouds are dark and ragged, although no rain falls from them. In some regions near the Equator, especially near lakes, heavy showers of convectional rain fall every afternoon. The showers usually last only a short time.

Rising air forms clouds, rain or snow

Sheltered or leeward slopes in rain shadow

Warm air carries water vapour above the clouds

Warm, dry air

HOW A MOUNTAIN RANGE CAUSES RELIEF RAINFALL

Relief rainfall

Relief rainfall occurs where warm winds carrying water vapour evaporated from the ocean meet a mountain range. The winds rise, the air cools and clouds form. These grow and cool as they rise, until they release rain or snow on the windward slopes of the mountains. On the far, or leeward, side, the winds blow downhill. They become warmer as they drop and evaporate moisture from the land. The leeward sides of mountains are often arid, or in a rain shadow.

This can have a dramatic effect on rainfall. The Andes Mountains separate southern Chile from Patagonia. Southern Chile is deluged by more than 2,500 mm of rain a year, whereas Patagonia often has less than 200 mm. The Great Basin Desert in Nevada has been formed as a result of a prolonged rain shadow effect. It is sheltered by the Sierra and Cascade ranges to the west, and the Rocky Mountains in the east.

RAIN OR DRIZZLE?

The difference between rain and drizzle is in the size of the raindrop, rather than how hard it is falling. Water drops with a diameter greater than 0.5 mm are classed as rain, whereas smaller drops are described as drizzle.

Air masses and fronts

The weather depends on where the air has come from, its temperature, and whether there are clouds. Much of the weather in the British Isles and Western Europe is caused by air masses from the Atlantic Ocean. One air mass can displace another. The boundaries between them are called fronts. The leading edge of a cold air mass is a cold front and of a warm air mass a warm front. Where one air mass is moved out of the way by another, the weather changes along the boundary or front.

Depressions

Depressions, or lows, are areas where the air pressure at the Earth's surface is low. They consist of light, warm, rising air. Depressions bring rain, storms and changing temperatures. Fresh masses of cold and warm air are constantly produced at the poles and the tropics, but the two do not mix easily. Depressions form along the polar front, where warm air from the tropics meets cold air from the poles. A wave develops along the boundary which forms a V-shape in which a wedge of warm air is trapped in the cool air. The warm air then rises, because it is less dense, creating a low pressure area.

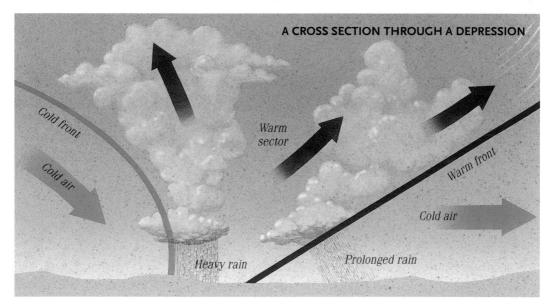

A CROSS SECTION THROUGH A DEPRESSION

Cold front

Cold air

Warm sector

Warm front

Cold air

Heavy rain

Prolonged rain

Winds blow into areas of low pressure from places with higher pressure. They are deflected by the Earth's rotation, turning anticlockwise in the northern hemisphere and clockwise in the southern. From a satellite, a depression appears as a mass of air which swirls like a stirred cup of tea. As the winds turn around it, the lighter warm air rises up and over the denser cold air. The front of the wedge of warm air is a warm front. There is a sequence of cloud, rain or snow, and temperature change as a warm front crosses an area. The dense cold air forces itself under the warm air from behind, forming a cold front with lower temperatures, heavy rain and storms.

A satellite photograph of a swirl of clouds which marks a depression over the North Atlantic. Parts of the United Kingdom and continental Europe are visible at the bottom right. Sometimes such depressions in the middle latitudes bring destructive gales and storms, especially in winter.

Occlusions

The wedge of warm air is gradually pushed higher and higher until it no longer touches the ground. Cold fronts move faster than warm fronts, and sometimes a cold front catches up with a warm front so the two merge. These are known as occluded fronts, or occlusions. Here the weather is unsettled, with cloud, rain and wind lasting for some time.

The path of a depression

You can usually tell when a depression is coming by the clouds that form. First to appear are cirrus clouds, then altocumulus, followed by stratus clouds. Last of all, at the cold front, come cumulonimbus, the big anvil-shaped rain clouds.

A depression moves along a path or track. Most travel north-easterly in the northern hemisphere and south-easterly in the southern. Weather forecasters try to predict these paths. Depressions last only a day or two, but often travel in families of three or four, with ridges of high pressure which bring short, sunny intervals between them.

Jet streams

About 10 to 15 km above the Earth, in the troposphere, are narrow, winding bands of very strong winds called jet streams, caused by the large differences in temperature between adjacent air masses along the polar front. The greater the difference in temperature, the stronger the jet stream; they can move at speeds of 480 kph.

Jet streams circle the Earth from west to east in both hemispheres. Where a jet stream bends away from the pole, it makes a trough where depressions form. Each jet stream steers the frontal depressions beneath it across the Atlantic and Pacific Oceans. Jet streams affect air travel. Over the Atlantic, they can slow down flights from Europe to North America or speed up flights in the opposite direction.

warm front

FRONTS

On a weather map, a warm front is shown by a line with red semicircles pointing in the direction of travel. A cold front is shown as a line with blue triangles pointing in the direction in which the front is going.

cold front

Thunderstorms

Thunderstorms sometimes occur on hot days when moist air close to the ground is heated and rises quickly. These rapidly rising air currents lead to the formation of towering cumulonimbus clouds with anvil-shaped tops. They may be only a few kilometres across and yet tower 20 km or so into the sky.

Inside a thundercloud, strong upward and downward air currents sweep ice crystals, ice pellets and water droplets past and into each other. These movements create static electricity which builds up in the cloud. Positive electric charges collect towards the top of the cloud and negative charges in the lower parts. The opposing electrical charges are strongly attracted to each other. Eventually the insulating layer of air between the two sets of charges cannot keep them apart and a massive spark – lightning – is released as the charges neutralise each other.

The lightning discharge can be within a cloud, between clouds, or between a cloud and the air. Only one in four lightning flashes travels from a cloud to the ground. Lightning is attracted to higher parts of the Earth's surface, which is why there are lightning conductors on high buildings and why it is dangerous to shelter under a tree in a thunderstorm. One of the safest places is inside a car, as the tyres provide insulation.

Sheet lightning within a cloud and cloud to ground lightning, two of the main types of lightning, are visible in this storm over south-east Arizona in the United States. Usually only about one in four lightning bolts reaches the ground.

Hailstorms are most common in the middle latitudes, but even here such large hailstones are unusual. Hail formation requires the strong updrafts associated with spring and summer storms.

Thunder and lightning

A lightning flash is hotter than 22,000°C. It superheats the air around it, making it expand at an incredible speed and then contract equally rapidly. This creates the sound waves we hear as thunder. Light travels faster than sound, so we see the lightning flash before we hear the thunder. The closer together they are, the nearer the storm. Light travels at 299,000 km per second, whereas it takes sound three seconds to travel a kilometre. Count the seconds between seeing lightning and hearing thunder, and divide by three, to calculate how many kilometres away a storm is.

What is hail?

Thunderclouds are so tall that their upper levels are well below freezing point. A raindrop on a strong rising current may be swept up so high that it freezes, only to fall again as the current weakens. At lower levels, the frozen raindrop may collect more water which freezes on the next upward thrust. This process can be repeated many times. Eventually spherical pellets of ice called hail fall to the ground.

Most are the size of peas, but in parts of central America and other middle latitudes, hailstones the size of golf or even tennis balls, can fall. Here hailstones with 25 layers of ice have been recorded. At this size they can wreak enormous damage.

metal canister

funnel

collecting tube

rainwater

rain

measure

MEASURING RAINFALL

Rain, and all other forms of precipitation, are collected in a rain gauge. It consists of a metal funnel that fits into the top of a cylindrical metal canister. Rain, frost, snow and hail are collected in the funnel and slide down into the small collecting tube. Every morning at 09.00, the collecting tube is lifted out carefully. Any snow, frost or hail is melted, and the water then poured into a measuring cylinder. Precipitation is usually measured in millimetres. Many rain gauges have a funnel 127 mm in diameter and are sunk into the ground so that the top of the funnel is 305 mm above the surface.

Snow and ice

7

A landscape covered with a thick layer of fresh snow is a beautiful sight. Snow is common during the winter months in Europe and northern North America and southern South America. Many mountaintops have a covering of snow, even near the Equator.

Ice crystals

Snowflakes are formed from tiny ice crystals in a cloud. They are created when water vapour freezes around minute solid particles in the middle and upper levels of the atmosphere, where temperatures are well below freezing point. Individual crystals join to make delicate hexagonal star shapes. They grow into triangles, columns or needles. The shape depends on the temperature and humidity of the air.

Melting snow

Snow falling from a cloud often melts on its way down and reaches the ground as rain. Snow may partially melt, or a mixture of snow and rain fall together as sleet when the temperature at ground level is just above freezing. As the falling snow melts, it takes heat from the surrounding air, lowering its temperature. This increases the chance that later falls of snow will reach the ground. Ideal conditions for snow are temperatures near or just below freezing point, rather than extremely cold. The warmer the snow, the more moisture it holds, and the bigger the snowflakes will be. Temperatures close to freezing point allow the snowflakes to melt, freeze again and join into larger flakes.

Heavy snowfalls and strong winds cause drifting which can block country roads.

Types of snow

Snowflakes formed in temperatures near freezing point are large and wet and tend to stick to surfaces. They are perfect for making snowballs! When air temperatures are well below freezing, snowflakes are small and powdery and ideal for skiing. Once snow has settled it may melt and freeze again, becoming harder and slippery to walk or drive on. The wind may blow snow into drifts against hedgerows and buildings. These can block roads and railways in exposed areas.

AMAZING SNOWFLAKES

German astronomer Johannes Kepler was the first to describe snowflakes accurately. In 1611 he discovered that nearly all ice crystals are six-sided and that no two are exactly alike.
An American farmer, Wilson Bentley (1865-1931) caught snowflakes on a black velvet-covered tray. He teased apart the individual ice crystals, smoothed them out with a feather and photographed each one magnified.

Wind-blown snow

Blizzards are snowstorms with strong winds which can damage telephone and power lines, leaving people without heat and light. The wind chill in a blizzard can be very dangerous for people out of doors. When blizzards hit Colorado in the United States in October 1997, the storms dropped 183 cm of snow in two days and killed 11 people. In Denver, the state capital, a thousand vehicles were abandoned.

Avalanches

A build-up of snow in mountain areas can lead to an avalanche. The most common kind of avalanche begins when an unstable mass of snow breaks away from a slope. As the snow gains speed it collects more snow, soil and rock. The whole mass rushes downhill at speeds which can reach 300 km per hour, destroying everything in its path.

An avalanche on Shispar Peak in Pakistan caused by fresh powdery snow breaking loose from older snow beneath.

Ice storms

Winter storms can also bring ice. Ice storms are formed when rain that has fallen through warmer air meets a layer of very cold air near the ground. The rain does not have time to change to sleet. Instead it turns to ice when it touches any solid object.

In January 1998, a severe ice storm lasting five days raged over eastern Canada and the north-eastern United States. More than 220,000 people lost their power supply in the state of Maine alone. The ice destroyed 2,500 pylons and brought down thousands of kilometres of cables. Falling trees and icy roads made travel almost impossible. In eastern Canada, the storm brought down 129,000 km of cables and 1,000 pylons, leaving three million people without power.

Black ice

Black ice is not black. It is glazed or clear ice which forms when rain or drizzle falls on a surface with a temperature below freezing point. It is difficult to see because it is clear and the road shows through.

8

Colourful skies

Our skies are an ever-changing display of colours. They include the rich blues of a cloud-free day, the reds, pinks and golds of sunrise and sunset and, occasionally, greens and purples. Many of these colours are created as a reaction between sunlight and water and dust in the atmosphere.

When the Sun is low in the sky, the path of its rays through the atmosphere is longer, and yellow, orange and red colours are scattered near the ground.

Colour and light

Although sunlight looks white, it is really made up of different wavelengths of light which have different colours. The colours are those we see in a rainbow – red, orange, yellow, green, blue, indigo and violet. Each colour travels at a different wavelength: red and orange have the longest wavelengths, while indigo and blue have the shortest.

As sunlight travels through the atmosphere, the light waves are scattered in different directions by dust, pollutants and the gas molecules that make up the air. The blue in sunlight is the most scattered and creates the blue sky we see on sunny days. We see the deepest blues when the air is dry, cold and clean. Water droplets and dust particles increase the scattering so that there are more green and yellow rays, which turn the sky a paler blue.

Sunrise, sunset and twilight

As the Sun rises or sets, its light has to travel further through the atmosphere, and through more cloud and dust, to reach our eyes. Much of the blue light is lost and more colours from the red and orange wavelengths are scattered, which creates the colours we see at the beginning or end of the day. Twilight is also the result of the scattering of light. As night approaches, we are not plunged into darkness, because of the dust and other impurities in the atmosphere. These particles scatter light from the sky and reflect it into the Earth's shadow, causing the soft rays of twilight after the Sun has set.

RED SKIES

During the mid-1880s, people in many parts of the world noticed that the sunsets were unusually red. They were caused by the greatest volcanic eruption in modern times – of Krakatoa in Indonesia in 1883. The gigantic explosion shot smoke and dust more than 50 km into the atmosphere, where it coloured the sunsets.

White clouds

Clouds are white because of the scattering of light by the water droplets from which they are made. In clouds the colours of the rainbow recombine to produce white light. If light does not pass through the cloud to the ground, or if another cloud casts a shadow, the clouds may appear grey or even black.

How rainbows form

When white light passes through a clear substance, such as glass or water, it is bent at a slight angle, or refracted. Colours of different wavelengths are refracted at slightly different angles, so the process causes the colours of white light to separate into bands called a spectrum. You sometimes see this array of colours when sunlight shines through a glass of water. You can see it even better if you shine white light through a triangular piece of glass called a prism.

A rainbow is created when raindrops refract sunlight. The raindrops act like minute prisms, and each colour emerges from a raindrop at a slightly different angle. The same colour emerges at the same angle from every one of the millions of raindrops in the cloud, so from the ground we see bands of colours – a spectrum in the sky.

The rainbow is part of a circle, but we usually see only the part above the horizon. You might see the full circle if you looked down on a rainbow from an aircraft. In a double rainbow the main rainbow has red at the top. The second, fainter rainbow has the colours in reverse order.

A rainbow is a spectrum in the sky. The colours are brightest at the foot because the largest raindrops are there.

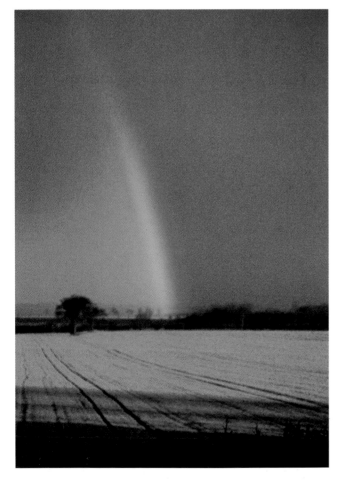

Haloes and coronas

A halo is the name for the luminous discs that sometimes appear round the Sun or, less often, the moon. Haloes are caused by the slight bending, or refraction, of light as it passes through a thin layer of high-level cloud made up of ice crystals. Similar effects, called coronas, appear when we see the Sun or moon through a thin layer of cloud made up of water droplets.

Northern and southern lights

The spectacular display of moving lights and colours created by the auroras are breathtaking. The auroras are called the northern lights, or aurora borealis, in the northern hemisphere and the southern lights, or aurora australis, in the southern hemisphere. They are most often seen in the polar regions, but you can see them at lower latitudes from time to time.

The auroras are created when the Sun emits fast-moving, electrically-charged particles, known as the solar wind. Most of the world, apart from the polar regions, is protected from these particles by the Earth's magnetic field. In the unprotected polar regions, the charged particles collide with the air molecules in the Earth's atmosphere. They give out energy in the form of red, green and white lights. These ascend in flickering sheets and streaks, roughly in the shape of a fan. The interaction between the solar wind and the air takes place between 150 km and 500 km above the Earth's surface.

LUCKY AURORA

Every year thousands of newly-wed Japanese couples travel to the small town of Yellowknife in Canada to watch the aurora borealis. They believe that seeing the aurora will bring good luck to their children. The aurora borealis used to be visible over Japan, but over the last 45 years or so it has drifted northwards.

Auroras, or northern and southern lights, are shimmering curtains of light caused when bursts of electrically-charged particles from the Sun enter the Earth's atmosphere. This display of the northern lights was in the sky over northern Norway.

Weather recording and forecasting

9

To make a weather forecast, meteorologists piece together information from thousands of weather stations and other sources across the world. When this information is compiled they can begin to predict what the weather will be like. Nowadays electronic instruments record much of the weather information automatically.

Collecting information

Temperature, pressure and rainfall figures are needed to forecast the weather, as well as wind speed and direction, humidity, visibility and the type, amount and height of the clouds. This information is collected day and night by thousands of people on land and at sea, and by automatic weather recording devices. Some ships carry equipment to record the weather conditions and weather buoys (either moored or drifting freely and powered by the Sun's energy), provide a continuous stream of information.

A weather station on top of an Austrian mountain. The white Stevenson screen protects the instruments from sunlight and radiation.

Weather stations

The simplest land-based weather station is a Stevenson screen. This wooden box on legs protects the instruments inside from sunlight and radiation from the ground. Air enters through the sides. Observers visit daily to copy down the information recorded. Today, most weather information is collected by small automatic stations on land around the world. They may be powered by the Sun and relay readings to forecasting centres by satellites.

Weather balloons

Weather forecasters also need to know the state of the atmosphere above the Earth's surface. One of the best ways of collecting this information is with a radiosonde. This is a package of instruments carried skywards by a helium-filled balloon.

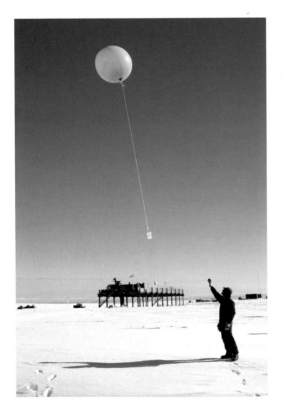

A scientist launching a radiosonde balloon at the Halley Research Station in Antarctica.

Radiosonde balloons are released several times a day from weather stations in many parts of the world. They are tracked by radar, which gives wind speed and direction, and contain a small radio transmitter which sends back details of the atmospheric pressure, temperature and humidity. At 20 km they burst and the package parachutes to Earth.

Aircraft and satellites

Many civil aircraft radio back weather information on intercontinental journeys. Meteorological satellites orbit the Earth, tracking the movements of hurricanes and collecting information in the upper atmosphere. Remote sensors on some measure sea temperatures, wave height, and even the thickness of sea-ice. Others carry radar that can show moving rain or snow.

There are two kinds of weather satellite. Geostationary satellites show the same part of the Earth's surface all the time. They remain above the same point on the Earth's surface, orbiting at the same speed. Others orbit the Earth, roughly from pole to pole. During a three day orbit, they send back a stream of pictures. Today land-based radar helps meteorologists monitor rain, snow and storms over an area.

Weather maps

Meteorologists publish their findings on a weather map called a synoptic chart, which is marked with symbols. This map shows isobars – lines joining places with the same atmospheric pressure. Barometer readings are marked in millibars or inches (1,000 mb = 29.54 inches). Anticyclones and depressions are marked 'high' (H) and 'low' (L) respectively, while symbols show the wind speed and direction. Bold lines mark warm and cold fronts, and half circles and spikes on them show the direction in which they are moving. On maps of the tropics, streamlines often represent the direction of travel of the weather.

A synoptic chart, which uses symbols to give a synopsis or summary of the weather over the United States at a particular time.

Changing weather patterns

10

The Earth's climate has changed many times since the Earth was formed about 4,600 million years ago. Sometimes the Earth has been much hotter than it is now; at other times much land has been covered by ice and snow during Ice Ages.

Fossil corals in this limestone found in Scotland, show that when the rock was formed the sediments settled in warm, shallow tropical seas. This shows that the British Isles were once much closer to the Equator.

Information from rocks

By studying layers of rocks, geologists can tell what the climate was like when they were formed. Sandstones and limestones are common rocks in the British Isles and North America. We know that sandstones were formed millions of years ago in ancient deserts, while limestones are largely composed of ancient corals and were formed in warm, shallow, tropical seas.

The last Ice Age

Tens of thousands of years ago early man lived in the grip of the last of the Ice Ages, which peaked about 18,000 years ago. Temperatures were several degrees lower than today and vast glaciers and ice sheets covered large parts of Europe, Scandinavia and North America. In the southern hemisphere, much of Argentina, New Zealand and parts of Australia and South Africa were also covered; about a third of the Earth's surface altogether. Stone Age paintings and engravings in caves in the Sahara Desert show that it was grassland during the last Ice Age and that lions, giraffes, elephants and hippopotamuses lived there. Sea levels were lower and people could walk from mainland Europe to what is now the British Isles, or from Russia to present-day USA.

This antelope carved by Stone Age people on the wall of a cave in the Sahara Desert in Algeria suggests that the area was once grassland.

The end of the Ice Age

The last Ice Age started to end about 12,000 years ago. The Earth began to warm and the ice to melt. As sea levels rose, early people became more isolated from each other. By about 7,000 years ago, the coastlines of the continents had begun to take on their present shape.

We now live in a warm period, but climatologists and historians have discovered that since the end of the last Ice Age there have been periods when it was warmer or cooler than today.

Modern-changes to climate

Scientists have many theories to explain these changes. Recent studies show that major volcanic eruptions can cause cold weather. The volcanic dust blocks out sunlight and so cools the Earth. Some scientists think that gradual changes in the Earth's orbit around the Sun or the tilt of its axis may have caused the climatic changes. These changes may have meant that the northern hemisphere received less of the Sun's heat than before, and so became colder.

Today, our weather is changing because of human activities. Weather changes include the formation of acid rain and photochemical smog, the growing hole in the ozone layer and global warming. These all result from our continued pollution of the atmosphere by wasteful industrial processes and fuel-inefficient methods of transport, from the Industrial Revolution onwards.

Acid rain

Acid rain describes the acidity of rain, and other forms of precipitation, including hail, sleet, snow, mist, fog and dew. Rainfall is always slightly acidic because carbon dioxide gas in the atmosphere dissolves in rainwater to form a weak acid called carbonic acid. However, burning

Scientists uncover a woolly mammoth from the ice in northern Russia. Mammoths became extinct 10,000 to 12,000 years ago. Micro-organisms and pollen grains preserved in the body tell us about the climate at that time.

fossil fuels, such as coal, oil and natural gas, produces waste gases, including sulphur dioxide and oxides of nitrogen. Combined with moisture in the atmosphere, these produce sulphuric and nitric acids and make the rain even more acid.

Acid rain damages freshwater fisheries, lakes, streams, groundwater, forests, crops, buildings, statues and human health. It is not a local problem. Once the acid gases reach the atmosphere, pollution may be carried thousands of kilometres. Acid rain produced by one country can damage the environment of another. The areas most at risk are in Europe and North America, but many parts of the world are threatened.

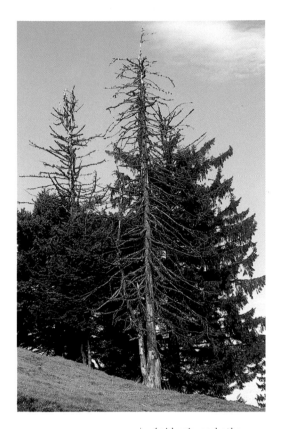

Acid rain and other pollutants are killing these conifers on a mountainside in Switzerland.

A police officer wears a mask as protection against the acid fumes while he directs traffic in South-East Asia.

The effects of smog

When there is fog in cities and industrial areas, particles of solid matter, especially from smoke, are trapped in the atmosphere. The resulting mixture of smoke and fog is known as smog. In persistent smogs, so much soot may accumulate in the fog that it is dangerous to breathe it. In December 1952, smog covered London and about 4,000 people were killed by the polluted air. Smogs are rare today because smokeless zones have been created and smoke from factories is better controlled.

A growing problem is the smog produced by vehicle exhausts. In some weather conditions, the exhaust gases emitted by vehicles cannot escape into the upper atmosphere. They produce a severe form of air pollution. Cities such as Los Angeles in the US and Mexico City are surrounded by hills. Calm weather traps vehicle fumes here and sunlight changes them into damaging ozone and choking smog. This type of pollution is called photochemical smog. In recent years much of India and South-East Asia has been affected by a brownish-coloured haze caused by fumes from traffic, power stations and factories and the smoke from fires used to clear forest areas. Air pollution of this kind leads to a huge increase in people with breathing problems such as asthma, bronchitis and lung infections.

The Antarctic ozone hole reaches a maximum each spring. The thinnest part of the ozone layer is shown in dark blue.

The ozone layer

Ozone is a form of oxygen in very small amounts in the atmosphere. The highest concentrations are in the stratosphere, about 20 to 25 km above the Earth's surface. Ozone has a number of roles. Most importantly, it shields the Earth's surface against ultraviolet radiation from the Sun. This would otherwise harm people, plants and animals.

Over the last 30 years, scientists measuring ozone levels over Antarctica and elsewhere have noticed that they are decreasing and that a hole is forming in the ozone layer. They believe the cause is a group of chemicals known as chlorofluorocarbons (CFCs). These were widely used in aerosols, refrigeration and air-conditioning units, dry cleaning, and the plastic foam used to make hamburger cartons. CFCs have now been banned in many countries but scientists think it will take 50 years for the ozone layer to repair itself.

Tropical rainforest is cleared by fire on the island of Borneo, Malaysia.

Global warming and the greenhouse effect

More and more scientists have produced evidence that the world's climate is becoming warmer. They believe this is due largely to pollution of the atmosphere.

Carbon dioxide is one of the gases that make up the air we breathe. Over the last 100 years, the amount in the atmosphere has increased, mainly because of the burning of fossil fuels and the clearance of forests by burning. Heat from the Sun is absorbed by the Earth's surface. Most of this heat is then radiated away from the Earth and some escapes back into space. Carbon dioxide and some other gases allow the Sun's energy to pass through to the Earth, but they trap the

GREENHOUSE GASES

There are more than 30 other greenhouse gases, including nitrous oxide, given out by fertilizers, exhausts and coal-fired power stations. This gas traps 270 times more heat than the same amount of carbon dioxide. Another greenhouse gas is methane, produced by microbes in swamps and by animal manure. It is also released when fossil fuels are burned and domestic waste is buried where it can rot. Other greenhouse gases include CFCs and ozone.

heat coming back from the surface of the Earth. They act in the same way as the glass in a greenhouse which retains warmth.The Earth needs this greenhouse effect. If gases such as carbon dioxide did not absorb some of the heat radiating from the Earth, the world would be colder. The oceans would freeze and the average temperature would be -18°C.

Until recently the world's natural levels of carbon dioxide had kept the Earth at a comfortable average temperature of 15°C. However, since the start of the Industrial Revolution people have been changing the composition of the atmosphere. We are building up a chemical blanket of carbon dioxide and other gases that trap more of the heat that used to escape. The result is an increase in temperature.

The effects of global warming

The world average temperature has risen by more than 0.5°C in the last 150 years. Scientists estimate that it could rise by up to 3°C by 2050 and up to 5.8°C by the end of the century. The last Ice Age was ended by a rise in temperature of only 3 or 4°C.

Most climatologists believe that the world's weather will continue to become more extreme, with more storms, hurricanes and tornadoes. Water will be scarcer in some places and sea levels will rise as polar ice melts. Islands and low lying cities will be flooded. Diseases such as malaria and cholera, and deaths from heat stroke and skin cancer will increase. Some crops will not grow where we grow them now. Crop yields will drop in some regions. Some plants and animals which cannot adapt will become extinct. You can read more about these changes in *Changing Climates*, another book in this series. Meanwhile, everyone can do their bit to help reduce the effects of climate change,

WHAT CAN WE DO?

We can all help to reduce the carbon dioxide and other greenhouse gases we produce. We can choose to use clean, renewable energy, such as wind, water or solar power, when they are available. We can walk, cycle or use public transport, rather than cars. We can recycle materials, insulate our homes and not waste electricity. We can use water supplies more carefully. Even small changes can make a difference.

Wind turbines create electricity without polluting the atmosphere.

Glossary

acid rain Rain that is more acid than usual because of the polluting gases from power stations and vehicle exhausts that are dissolved in it.

advection fog Fog formed when warm, moist air passes over a cooler surface.

air pressure The force of the air pressing down on the Earth's surface.

anemometer An instrument for measuring wind speed.

anticyclone A large area of high pressure (sometimes called a high) from which all winds blow outwards.

atmosphere The blanket of gases around a planet, held there by the pull of the planet's gravity.

aurora Bands of coloured lights that appear in the sky. In the northern hemisphere they are called the northern lights or the aurora borealis, in the southern hemisphere they are called the southern lights or aurora australis.

avalanche A rapid movement of snow, sometimes combined with ice and rock material, down a steep slope.

barometer An instrument for measuring air pressure.

blizzard Severe weather conditions combining heavy snow, strong winds, low temperatures and poor visibility.

climate The average weather in a place over a long period of time.

clouds Masses of water droplets or ice particles floating in the atmosphere. There are ten types of cloud, with three basic groups: stratus, cumulus and cirrus.

condensation The process by which a vapour or gas changes into a liquid as it cools.

Coriolis effect The way that the direction of winds is turned by the spin of the Earth – to the right in the northern hemisphere and to the left in the southern hemisphere. The Coriolis force is strongest at the poles and weakens towards the Equator, where it disappears altogether.

current A body of air or water moving in a definite direction.

cyclone (see hurricane)

depression An area of low pressure, sometimes called a low, which brings unsettled weather. It may also be called a cyclone.

dew point The temperature at which water vapour in the air will condense.

evaporation The process by which a liquid is changed into a vapour or gas when it is heated.

fossil fuel A fuel produced from the fossil remains of plants or animals: coal, peat, oil or natural gas.

front The boundary between two masses of air at different temperatures. Rain often occurs along a front.

global warming The warming of the Earth's atmosphere as a result of air pollution.

greenhouse effect The warming of the Earth, caused by certain gases in the atmosphere, called greenhouse gases. These allow the Sun's rays to reach the Earth's surface, but trap heat given off by the ground.

humidity The amount of water vapour in the air.

hurricane A violent tropical storm in the Caribbean and North Atlantic with winds blowing at 118 km/h or more around a low pressure centre. It is known as a typhoon in the north-western Pacific and a cyclone in the Indian Ocean and around Australia.

Ice Age One of several periods in the Earth's history when huge glaciers and ice sheets covered large parts of the land surface.

ice storm A storm in which falling rain freezes as soon as it touches any object which is below freezing point.

jet stream A narrow band of very strong winds in the upper levels of the troposphere.

meteorology The study of how the atmosphere creates the weather and climate.

monsoon A wind which blows from different directions at different times of the year, causing wet and dry seasons, particularly in southern Asia, northern Australia and western Africa.

occlusion The condition of the atmosphere when an advancing cold front overtakes a warm front, raising the warm sector of the depression and cutting it off from the Earth's surface.

ozone layer A layer of ozone gas (a form of oxygen) in the Earth's atmosphere which absorbs 90 per cent of the harmful ultra-violet rays from the Sun.

polar front The boundary (or front) between warm tropical air and cold polar air in the middle latitudes north and south of the Equator. Frontal depressions form and travel along it.

precipitation Any form of water (solid or liquid) that falls from the atmosphere and reaches the ground.

prevailing wind The main direction from which the wind blows in particular places.

radiation fog Fog that forms at night in low-lying areas when the air is moist, the sky is clear and there is little wind. The ground cools quickly, cooling the air above.

rain shadow An area of decreased rainfall on the lee, or sheltered, side of a hill or mountain.

relative humidity The ratio between the actual amount of water vapour in the air and the maximum amount it can hold at a given temperature.

relief rainfall Rainfall resulting from hills and mountains causing clouds to rise and cool.

snow-line The lowest level on a mountain above which snow never disappears.

spectrum Bands of colours like those seen in a rainbow, formed by splitting white light into its constituent colours.

stratosphere The layer of the atmosphere that lies above the troposphere.

synoptic chart A weather chart that provides detailed information about weather conditions at a particular time over a large area.

tornado An intense, rotating column of air, shaped like a funnel or rope, that extends down from the base of a cloud to the ground.

trade wind Steady winds in the tropics blowing from the north-east in the northern hemisphere and from the south-east in the southern hemisphere.

tree-line The highest point at which trees grow on a mountain.

troposphere The layer of the atmosphere that is closest to the Earth. This is where our weather occurs.

ultraviolet rays Invisible rays given off by the Sun and other very hot objects. Ultraviolet rays can burn the skin and cause skin cancer.

vacuum A completely empty space without air in it.

water cycle The continuous circulation of water from the Earth's surface to the atmosphere, involving evaporation, condensation and precipitation.

waterspout A rotating column of air that extends downwards from the base of a cloud to touch a water surface. It is usually less violent than a tornado.

water vapour Water in the form of an invisible gas.

Index